Yield to the Willow

Yield to the Willow

Don Wentworth

[signature]

Six Gallery Press

Acknowledgments

Some of the poems in this collection appeared, occasionally in a slightly different form, in the following publications:

bear creek haiku, bottle rockets, Bright Star, Cattails: Journal of the United Haiku and Tanka Society, Cotyledon, frogpond, Lummox, The Margarine Maypole Orangutan Express, Mockersatz, Modern Haiku, The New Yinzer, Penny Dreadful Review, Per Diem (Haiku Foundation), *The Pittsburgh Post-Gazette, Poetalk, Rolling Stone, So It Goes: The Journal of the Kurt Vonnegut Memorial Library, tinywords, Troutswirl, Wild Plum, word pond,* and the anthologies *fear of dancing: The Red Moon Anthology of English-Language Haiku 2013, Haiku 21: an Anthology of Contemporary English-Language Haiku* (Revised edition), *Standing Still: Haiku North America,* and *The Temple Bell Stops: Contemporary Poems of Grief and Loss*

Special thanks to Joy McCall, Che Elias, Nathan Kukulski, and Evan Swanson.

for Laurie ... always

Introduction

Mystics have long known that the only way to perceive the essence of anything is through separation. In the language of kabbalists each letter is possessed by its own unique energy. Each letter is represented by a symbol that illustrates its function. The symbol for the letter Zayin is the sword. The sword is the energy that cuts through, that separates the illusions of this world in order to sanctify.

In feudal Japan when the era of the samurai was waning many left the warrior class to become monks. Yet these monks, offspring of generations of warriors, did not surrender the great gift of the sword. Bashō himself hailed from samurai stock.

The innate knowledge of the way of the sword, unified with the contemplative practice of Zen, was to have a profound influence upon poetry. Haiku laid waste the bullshit. The practice of refining the short poem became an art form. Its power spread. It morphed with similar literary forms far from Japan. The tradition continues to evolve.

Today the short poem reveals the essence of things as much or more than any art form upon the planet. Ever.

You hold here a copy of *Yield to the Willow*, a collection of short poetry composed by Don Wentworth, a man who has devoted his life to the practice of the short poem—not only through study and writing, but also with the higher labor of love: editing. This is rare. In every aspect, Don Wentworth is a master of the short poem.

Wield this book carefully for it is sharper than a samurai sword. Yield to the willow, indeed!

~ Charlie Mehrhoff

Yield to the willow
All the loathing, all the desire
Of your heart

~ *Bashō*
translated by R. H. Blyth

Everything that is is music.
All that is needed is
that it should be heard.

~ Romain Rolland
translated by Gilbert Cannan

this, too, shall pass —
living day-to-day

just beyond reach
just within reach
everything

morning glory
opens to anything,
even you

ant circling the bindweed,
ant circling the bindweed,
ant circling the bindweed —

write it yourself

without love,
dewdrops
ignored

how the worm
swings as the robin
hops, oh,
how the worm
swings

swings

spring maple key to my heart

The Ten-Thousand and First Thing

What is it about the silence
that surrounds the heron in the pond,
and this human watching the heron,
and that world drifting leisurely,
on one leg, through fixed eternity?

the sound of one gull
overwhelms the sea

a robin
walking across the street
as if there's a choice

My life,—
How much more of it remains?
The night is brief.

~ Shiki
translated by R. H. Blyth

just one word
and, yes, no syllables
left

Sutra Blues

the haunted man
needs no house

You say you're lost
but look, see —
Mister Ant
knows
the
way

fool, fool,
listen to the fool —
sparrow does

I will not bow,
so, as always,
creation
rises
up

pleading, begging, praying —
yet, the sun sets
in the west

hazy distant moon
both of us moving
across the sky

still searching
for that one word —
weeping willow
at dusk

spiteful and ungenerous,
the blue jay
knows you

earth to the river
river to the sea
sea to the sky
to you
to me

*Any man is more than
the greatest of books.*

~ George MacDonald

on the same branch
cherry blossom, snow dollop
I and I

Long After Issa

Watch out, ants —
clumsy sinner
with big feet!

sparrow's little singing lesson: be, leave

The Disappearance of Myth

whosoever dares to doubt
a haunting, creates
a ghost

mid-December
even pear & gingko give it up —
biopsy positive

postwar home
gone — lingering,
the lilac scent

even
when no moon —
moon

Prelude to the High Wire

If you were Marc Chagall
on a swing & I was a passing
angel, the houses would fall
away faster than the wings
of love might part
the waiting air

one noble truth leaf after leaf after leaf

presumptuous
thinking the Buddhist way
presumptuous

There are eleven great planetary gyres.

~ Ruth Ozeki

not quite right the perfect note

morning glory
threading barbed wire —
blossom, you fool!

brisk west wind,
yet the meadow grass sways
both ways

each night now
shorter than the one before —
beautiful willow
stirring, barely —
the silence

recycling, too, the plastic begonias

locust tree
gone from the bus stop

how much longer
the wait

So, yes, & now, before
we kill it, before we eradicate,
obliterate it, we must bow down
to thank it — cancer, that is —
for, as you will see,
it, too, plays
its part

all day long
the sparrow, the sparrow
the cellphone
the cellphone

coming through cracks
in the cement everywhere
this poem

hanging low
so beautiful
the willow
rhyming
with the
stream

The House of Rain

Butterfly, these words
From my brush are not flowers
only their shadows

~ Soseki
translated by Harry Behn

the big picture —
sunset, butterfly

writing haiku
while I walk, I arrive
before I know it —

but where?

slime trail —
glancing back at
the glinting

from Woody Guthrie's 1942
New Year's Resolution List

31. Love everybody.
32. Make up your mind.
33. Wake up and fight.

walking from the grave
with the answer & question
forever bound

not one
original thought sings
robin robin
red breast
red breast

We assume
the butterfly is
sleepy —
the butterfly assumes
nothing at all

After Li Po's *A Farewell Song of White Clouds*

I follow the white clouds.
The white clouds follow me.
Everywhere we go, we move together,
even as we drift apart.

Tell me, my friend, what is it, exactly,
about rain that you don't understand?

every year, sparrow
returns — different sparrow,
same return

silence falls, too,
on the roof of the house
of rain

Nothing is my last word about anything.

~ Henry James

First World problem:
learning to shut
your fucking
mouth

on the side
of the collapsing barn —
"Chew"

no time like the present no time

near frozen rain
beads on the leafless maple —
so, too, with love
each perfect little drop
refracts the light

in the meadow
everything, eventually,
comes to you

among the 10,000 things —
August silence

on the ground,
the bruised apricot —
cancer, too,
is life

The Butterfly Affect

Focusing on the dainty powerful motion
of the gold black wings of a butterfly
we miss the fact that it has settled on
the corner of an advertising sign on
the marble floor of the cavernous hall
of Grand Central Station in the city
of New York on a spinning planet
threading through a universe likewise
in motion and we: we are on our way

holding a little blue
plastic bag of crap

you know what
you know

that slow lope,
of nowhere to go,
been there, everywhere, before —
look, see, the willow
yields to you

Orchidectomy

*Haiku is like a finger pointing at
the moon. Once you've seen it,
you no longer need the finger.*

*~ Variation of an aphorism by
Sixth Zen Patriarch, Hui-Neng*

hiding in everything plain sight

leaning over,
whispering in my ear,
cancer says,
here, take my hand,
let's walk

half a world apart —
different crazies
same moon

kitten
stinking of lilac
fooling no one

A Single, Fluted Feather   *for Angele Ellis*

To those who would despair of all things human
I give you the robin on the ground, scurrying,
stopping - looking - pausing - starting again.

To those ebullient with mankind's immense potential,
I give you the poplar tree, the makeshift gallows,
the foreign detention center, the ubiquitous ovens.

To those who are just plain confused,
I give you the sudden snap of wings,
the robin in flight, now lighting

on the thinnest branch of all.

America, America

so impatient
I can't wait
to die

fresh snow cupped
in a torn white blossom —
orchidectomy

The History of Western Literature

So here it is, a person,
a woman, a life,
reduced to a
single poem.

& there, there they are,
all of them, all of
us, getting it
wrong.

at the church
the mortician smokes
while he waits

even in stillness the buoy bell

As long as the world keeps on turning,
I keep on turning, too

~ Bob Dylan

breath or breeze the leaf will move

chirping cardinal
your lips forming
the words

forcing a poem
its petals all over
the ground

After Issa

today also,
today also, the lone man
answers himself,
answers himself

each more beautiful
than the next
unfurling
humans

no matter the angle
of the tiger lily how
the pistils
all curve
up

burnt umber tip
of the dogwood blossom —
penile lesion

3 words extracted from the script of
a 30 second commercial on a
"You give us 22 minutes, we'll give you the world"
all-news channel

death   insurance   guarantee

the distance
between father and son walking
connects them

today, just letting it be —
wildflower
picks
you

The Yellow Door

The mind has its landscapes and only a short time is allowed for their contemplation.

~ Marcel Proust
translated by Ian Patterson

here, here is my begging bowl
come take from it
what you will

only when
they stop talking, you know —
August cicadas

even as it opens,
a new petal falling —
day 4, radiation

on our knees
in the garden, snail and I
watch each other closely
the yellow door
slightly ajar

awakening
to another world
everyone still here

full moon
quickly waning like me
just like you

gathering
wild flowers
in the meadow
the meadow
gathers
us

long winter —
covered in snow
the snow shovel

plain speaking —
still robin makes
her point

leaving
my shadow shows
the way

*Poetry never forgets the all
even when it is dealing with
exclusively one thing.*

~ R. H. Blyth

holding
the mirror up for you
I see myself

only the dying
truly alive
you dumb
fuck
you

in a small stoppered tube
two baby teeth —
the first crocus

crisp autumn morning
the treetop cardinal
doesn't want
anything

Guardian Self Storage indeed

head tucked just so,
beautiful sparrow,
dead on the ground

looking down,
at foreskin, bunching up:
my father, uncut,
alive

both sides
of the leaf as it falls —
chemical castration

pressing the button
for the floor I'm on
I arrive

The Nightmare

Wake up!

You're not dreaming.

The Lark Replies

Before the white chrysanthemum,
  the scissors hesitate
  a moment

~ Buson
translated by R. H. Blyth

freeing centipede
trapped in the tub
I step inside
myself

put out the light
turn on the moon,
my love, turn on
the moon

for Laurie

watching
the phone ring
all history
trembling
before you

feeling for the hair
which is not loose
the 2nd Noble truth

sly puppet
in the fortune teller's box —
nobody owns the moon

On Elitism

Walking about, you might stumble on a meadow
full of daisies when emerging from a darkened
wood. All seem the same; all quite lovely, having a
collective presence, a certain oneness.

Cutting through the meadow, you see in the near
distance a road, perhaps one you've taken before.
There is a ditch, or trench, that runs along the
side of the road, and there is a single daisy, near
an adjoining culvert, in its full splendor.

This daisy stands out, errant though it may be. You
- we - are attracted to it: it seems, somehow, finer
than the rest.

Behind us now is the meadow, resplendent with
daisies. Ahead, a ditch, with a single daisy, a daisy
that stands out.

> every
> single
> petal
>
> every
> one

grief
brings so much
and more —
the first robin
after the storm

for Joy McCall

After Lenore Kandel

'Losing faith
in the morning,' she says
& the lark replies

no need to tell
what it is you mutter to yourself
Mister Crow

no here there dragonfly

Nothing has been, nothing will be;
everything is, everything has
essence and presence.

~ Hermann Hesse
translated by Ralph Manheim

bits of grit & oh oil in the ash

before the light
on a nearby snowdrop expires,
you've changed

taking the healing cds
to the 2nd hand shop —
numinous twilight

thin skinned, Sister Death
goodbye to *you*, too,
goodbye

wearing the gear teeth down —
hearing father's voice
slipping away

emptiness
in a shimmering drop of dew
dancing

in memory,
in the moment,
always

rheumy eyed bastard
on the library steps —

Mister Bodhisattva
to you

hole in the center
of the snowflake
another koan
revealed

tulips
even when not moving
moving

The written word is a lie.

~ Johnny Lydon

pecking the red spot
where sparrow's head once was —
Brother Sparrow

'nice little rigor'
says the facilitator
a cloud
slipping in front
of the moon

Wearing the insect mask
to prevent insect murder.

Who will wear the human mask?

let this cup pass —
but, if not,
one slow
sweet
sip

a gentle breeze
praying mantis among
the green beans
eat & be
eaten

all the skinny nurses
smoking behind the hospital
know all
about that wine
'spo-dee-oo-dee'

in every light rain,
between the drops,
the sure soft
steps of my
dear, dead
friend

for Huff

fixing makeup
in the ATM screen —
withdrawal time

Seen on a church marquee, as is:

Living Your
Deepest Desire
Retreat

dictating
the definition of poetry,
you wild daisies you

The wanton boy who kills a fly
Shall feel the spider's enmity

~ *William Blake*

Grand Unified Theory

the moment
becomes
you

wind
blowing through zazen
leaves

Winter Sonata

Look, see her hands
as she watches
the swallows
move

chatting on the porch —
two sparrows flitting
in autumn mist

for Laurie

Just
as you're wiping your ass:
that thought

sound-alike product: Amerika

Towards the Biography of a Terrorist

In the news clip, a man strides onto a balcony,
half-turning to a young boy. His hand swiftly
shoots out, tousles the boy's hair & then, with

a palm to a forehead, like a holy man, he gives
him a gentle shove, thick fingers gliding down
the boy's angelic face & two winged smiles.

detritus
of 100 billion dead —
how slowly, slowly
the earth
turns

in harsh light
metal petals slowly closing,
peeling open —
with you, cancer,
smiling at the center

December rhododendron not waiting

A bath when you're born,
a bath when you die,
how stupid.

~ Issa
translated by Robert Hass

the known not knowing
December sparrow

if you got the time
I've got the poem —
rhododendron
bud

this baggage
still so heavy
after its unpacked

buttercup
under the chin
a different yellow

off the consulting room,
the psychiatrist's
private entrance

not sure if
there are fewer flags
or more soldiers —
poppy fields
paved with words

little twitch and gone ... this world

arriving before you thought —
this old man smell

cherry blossoms
in front of the cancer center —
the automated reminder

never again,
never again,
always

Coda

The thing my sister and I loved best was when somebody in a movie would tell everybody off, then make a grand exit into a coat closet. He had to come out again, of course, all tangled in coat hangers and scarves.

~ Kurt Vonnegut

even, yet, still, too —
the haiku poet fooling
himself

while
everyone studies Buddhism
crow waits

mid-summer
killing the firefly
seeking the light

above the empty shells
below the sycamores —
singing cicadas

not one poem
this cherry blossom season
yet all these petals

after
stumbling on the acorn
seeing the oak

peeing on a roach is one way
the roach eating you is another

nothing is mutually exclusive

beyond the maxim
the meadow
still

work the room
whispers the wind to the pine
& the river answers yes

begin
at the beginning
glistening maggot